Chapter 1 - God

We confess and acknowledge one God alone, to whom alone we must cleave, whom alone we must serve, whom only we must worship, and in whom alone we put our trust. Who is eternal, infinite, immeasurable, incomprehensible, omnipotent, invisible; one in substance and yet distinct in three persons, the Father, the Son, and the Holy Ghost. By whom we confess and believe all things in heaven and earth, visible and invisible to have been created, to be retained in their being, and to be ruled and guided by his inscrutable providence for such end as his eternal wisdom, goodness, and justice have appointed, and to the manifestation of his own glory.

Chapter 2 - The Creation of Man

We confess and acknowledge that our God has created man, i.e.., our first father, Adam, after his own image and likeness, to whom he gave wisdom, lordship, justice, free will, and self-consciousness, so that in the whole nature of man no imperfection could be found. From this dignity and perfection man and woman both fell; the woman being deceived by the serpent and man obeying the voice of the woman, both conspiring against the sovereign majesty of God, who in clear words had previously threatened death if they presumed to eat of the forbidden tree.

Chapter 3 - Original Sin

By this transgression, generally known as original sin, the image of God was utterly defaced in man, and he and his children became by nature hostile to God, slaves to Satan, and servants to sin. And thus everlasting death has had, and shall have, power and dominion over all who have not been, are not, or shall not be born from above. This rebirth is wrought by the power of the Holy Ghost creating in the hearts of God's chosen ones an assured faith in the promise of God revealed to us in his Word; by this faith we grasp Christ Jesus with the graces and blessings promised in him.

Chapter 4 - The Revelation of the Promise

We constantly believe that God, after the fearful and horrible departure of man from his obedience, did seek Adam again, call upon him, rebuke and convict him of his sin, and in the end made unto him a most joyful promise, that "the seed of the woman should bruise the head of the serpent," that is, that he should destroy the works of the devil. This promise was repeated and made clearer from time to time; it was embraced with joy, and most constantly received by all the faithful from Adam to Noah, from Noah to Abraham, from Abraham to David, and so onwards to the incarnation of Christ Jesus; all (we mean the believing fathers under the law) did see the joyful day of Christ Jesus, and did rejoice.

Chapter 5 - The Continuance, Increase, and Preservation of the Kirk

We most surely believe that God preserved, instructed, multiplied, honored, adorned, and called from death to life his Kirk in all ages since Adam until the coming of Christ Jesus in the flesh. For he called Abraham from his father's country, instructed him, and multiplied his seed, he marvelously preserved him, and more marvelously delivered his seed from the bondage and tyranny of Pharaoh; to them he gave his laws, constitutions, and ceremonies; to them he gave the land of Canaan; after he had given them judges, and afterwards Saul, he gave David to be king, to whom he gave promise that of the fruit of his loins should one sit forever upon his royal throne. To this same people from time to time he sent prophets, to recall them to the right way of their God, from which sometimes they strayed by idolatry. And although, because of their stubborn contempt for righteousness he was compelled to give them into the hands of their enemies, as had previously been threatened by the mouth of Moses, so that the holy city was destroyed, the temple burned with fire, and the whole land desolate for seventy years, yet in mercy he restored them again to Jerusalem, where the city and the temple were rebuilt, and they endured against all temptations and assaults of Satan till the Messiah came according to the promise.

Chapter 6 - The Incarnation of Jesus Christ

When the fullness of time came God sent his Son, his eternal wisdom, the substance of his own glory, into this world, who took the nature of humanity from the substance of a woman, a virgin, by means of the Holy Ghost. And so was born the "just seed of David," the "Angel of the great counsel of God," the very Messiah promised, whom we confess and acknowledge to be Emmanuel, true God and true man, two perfect natures united and joined in one person. So by our Confession, we condemn the damnable and pestilent heresies of Arius, Marcion, Eutyches, Nestorius, and such others as did either deny the eternity of his Godhead, or the truth of his humanity, or confounded them, or else divided them.

Chapter 7 - Why the Mediator Had to Be True God and True Man

We acknowledge and confess that this wonderful union between the Godhead and the humanity in Christ Jesus did arise from the eternal and immutable decree of God from which all our salvation springs and depends.

Chapter 8 - Election

That same eternal God and Father, who by grace alone chose us in his Son Christ Jesus before the foundation of the world was laid, appointed him to be our head, our brother, our pastor, and the great bishop of our souls. But since the opposition between the justice of God and our sins was such that no flesh by itself could or might have attained unto God, it behooved the Son of God to descend unto us and take himself a body of our body, flesh of our flesh, and bone of our bone, and so become the Mediator between God and man, giving power to as many as believe in him to be the sons of God; as he himself says, "I ascend to my Father and to your Father, to my God and to your God." By this most holy brotherhood whatever we have lost in Adam is restored to us again. Therefore we are not afraid to call God our Father, not so much because he has created us, which we have in common with the reprobate, as because he has given unto us his only Son to be our brother, and given us grace to acknowledge and embrace him as our only Mediator. Further, it behooved the Messiah and Redeemer to be true God and true man, because he was able to undergo the punishment of our transgressions and to present himself in the presence of his Father's judgment, as in our stead, to suffer for our transgression and disobedience, and by death to overcome him that was the author of death. But because the Godhead alone could not suffer death, and neither could manhood overcome death, he joined both together in one person, that the weakness of one should suffer and be subject to death--which we had deserved--and the infinite and invincible power of the other, that is, of the Godhead, should triumph, and purchase for us life, liberty, and perpetual victory. So we confess, and most undoubtedly believe.

Chapter 9 - Christ's Death, Passion, and Burial

That our Lord Jesus offered himself a voluntary sacrifice unto his Father for us, that he suffered contradiction of sinners, that he was wounded and plagued for our transgressions, that he, the clean innocent Lamb of God, was condemned in the presence of an earthly judge, that we should be absolved before the judgment seat of our God; that he suffered not only the cruel death of the cross, which was accursed by the sentence of God; but also that he suffered for a season the wrath of his Father which sinners had deserved. But yet we avow that he remained the only, well beloved, and blessed Son of his Father even in the midst of his anguish and torment which he suffered in body and soul to make full atonement for the sins of his people. From this we confess and avow that there remains no other sacrifice for sin; if any affirm so, we do not hesitate to say that they are blasphemers against Christ's death and the everlasting atonement thereby purchased for us.

Chapter 10 - The Resurrection

We undoubtedly believe, since it was impossible that the sorrows of death should retain in bondage the Author of life, that our Lord Jesus crucified, dead, and buried, who descended into hell, did rise again for our justification, and the destruction of him who was the author of death and its bondage. We know that his resurrection was confirmed by the testimony of his enemies, and by the resurrection of the dead, whose sepulchers did open, and they did rise and appear to many within the city of Jerusalem. It was also confirmed by the testimony of his angels, and by the senses and judgment of his apostles and of others, who had conversation, and did eat and drink with him after his resurrection.

Chapter 11 - The Ascension

We do not doubt but that the selfsame body which was born of the virgin, was crucified, dead, and buried, and which did rise again, did ascend into the heavens, for the accomplishment of all things, where in our name and for our comfort he has received all power in heaven and earth, where he sits at the right hand of the Father, having received his kingdom, the only advocate and mediator for us. Which glory, honor, and prerogative, he alone amongst the brethren shall possess till all his enemies are made his footstool, as we undoubtedly believe they shall be in the Last Judgment. We believe that the same Lord Jesus shall visibly return for this Last Judgment as he was seen to ascend. And then, we firmly believe, the time of refreshing and restitution of all things shall come, so that those who from the beginning have suffered violence, injury, and wrong, for righteousness' sake, shall inherit that blessed immortality promised them from the beginning. But, one the other hand, the stubborn, disobedient, cruel persecutors, filthy persons, idolaters, and all sorts of the unbelieving, shall be cast into the dungeon of utter darkness, where their worm shall not die, nor their fire be quenched. The remembrance of that day, and of the Judgment to be executed in it, is not only a bridle by which our carnal lusts are restrained but also such inestimable comfort that neither the threatening of worldly princes, nor the fear of present danger or of temporal death, may move us to renounce and forsake that blessed society which we, the members, have with our Head and only Mediator, Christ Jesus: whom we confess and avow to be the promised Messiah, the only Head of his Kirk, our just Lawgiver, our only High Priest, Advocate, and Mediator. To which honors and offices, if man or angel presume to intrude themselves, we utterly detest and abhor them, as blasphemous to our sovereign and supreme Governor, Christ Jesus.

Chapter 12 - Faith in the Holy Ghost

Our faith and its assurance do not proceed from flesh and blood, that is to say, from natural powers within us, but are the inspiration of the Holy Ghost; whom we confess to be God, equal with the Father and with his Son, who sanctifies us, and brings us into all truth by his own working, without whom we should remain forever enemies to God and ignorant of his Son, Christ Jesus. For by nature we are so dead, blind, and perverse, that neither can we feel when we are pricked, see the light when it shines, nor assent to the will of God when it is revealed, unless the Spirit of the Lord Jesus quicken that which is dead, remove the darkness from our minds, and bow our stubborn hearts to the obedience of his blessed will. And so, as we confess that God the Father created us when we were not, as his Son our Lord Jesus redeemed us when we were enemies to him, so also do we confess that the Holy Ghost does sanctify and regenerate us, without respect to any merit proceeding from us, be it before or after our regeneration. To put this even more plainly; as we willingly disclaim any honor and glory from our own creation and redemption, so do we willingly also for our regeneration and sanctification; for by ourselves we are not capable of thinking one good thought, but he who has begun the work in us alone continues us in it, to the praise and glory of his undeserved grace.

Chapter 13 - The Cause of Good Works

The cause of good works, we confess, is not our free will, but the Spirit of the Lord Jesus, who dwells in our hearts by true faith, brings forth such works as God has prepared for us to walk in. For we most boldly affirm that it is blasphemy to say that Christ abides in the hearts of those in whom is no spirit of sanctification. Therefore we do not hesitate to affirm that murderers, oppressors, cruel persecutors, adulterers, filthy persons, idolaters, drunkards, thieves, and all workers of iniquity, have neither true faith nor anything of the Spirit of the Lord Jesus, so long as they obstinately continue in wickedness. For as soon as the Spirit of the Lord Jesus, whom God's chosen children receive by true faith, takes possession of the heart of any man, so soon does he regenerate and renew him, so that he begins to hate what before he loved, and to love what he hated before. Thence comes that continual battle which is between the flesh and Spirit in God's children, while the flesh and the natural man, being corrupt, lust for things pleasant and delightful to themselves, are envious in adversity and proud in prosperity, and every moment prone and ready to offend the majesty of God. But the Spirit of God, who bears witness to our spirit that we are the sons of God, makes us resist filthy pleasures and groan in God's presence for deliverance from this bondage of corruption, and finally to triumph over sin so that it does not reign in our mortal bodies. Other men do not share this conflict since they do not have God's Spirit, but they readily follow and obey sin and feel no regrets, since they act as the devil and their corrupt nature urge. But the sons of God fight against sin; sob and mourn when they find themselves tempted to do evil; and, if they fall, rise again with earnest and unfeigned repentance. They do these things, not by their own power, but by the power of the Lord Jesus, apart from whom they can do nothing.

Chapter 14 - The Works Which Are Counted Good Before God

We confess and acknowledge that God has given to man his holy law, in which not only all such works as displease and offend his godly majesty are forbidden, but also those which please him and which he has promised to reward are commanded. These works are of two kinds. The one is done to the honor of God, the other to the profit of our neighbor, and both have the revealed word of God as their assurance. To have one God, to worship and honor him, to call upon him in all our troubles, to reverence his holy Name, to hear his Word and to believe it, and to share in his holy sacraments, belong to the first kind. To honor father, mother, princes, rulers, and superior powers; to love them, to support them, to obey their orders if they are not contrary to the commands of God, to save the lives of the innocent, to repress tyranny, to defend the oppressed, to keep our bodies clean and holy, to live in soberness and temperance, to deal justly with all men in word and deed, and, finally, to repress any desire to harm our neighbor, are the good works of the second kind, and these are most pleasing and acceptable to God as he has commanded them himself. Acts to the contrary are sins, which always displease him and provoke him to anger, such as, not to call upon him alone when we have need, not to hear his Word with reverence, but to condemn and despise it, to have or worship idols, to maintain and defend idolatry, lightly to esteem the reverend name of God, to profane, abuse, or condemn the sacraments of Christ Jesus, to disobey or resist any whom God has placed in authority, so long as they do not exceed the bounds of their office, to murder, or to consent thereto, to bear hatred, or to let innocent blood be shed if we can prevent it. In conclusion, we confess and affirm that the breach of any other commandment of the first or second kind is sin, by which God's anger and displeasure are kindled against the proud, unthankful world. So that we affirm good works to be those alone which are done in faith and at the command of God who, in his law, has set forth the things that please him. We affirm that evil works are not only those expressly done against God's command, but also, in religious matters and the worship of God, those things which have no other warrant than the invention and opinion of man. From the beginning God has rejected such, as we learn from the words of the prophet Isaiah and of our master, Christ Jesus, "In vain do they worship Me, teaching the doctrines and commandments of men."

Chapter 15 - The Perfection of the Law and The Imperfection of Man

We confess and acknowledge that the law of God is most just, equal, holy, and perfect, commanding those things which, when perfectly done, can give life and bring man to eternal felicity; but our nature is so corrupt, weak, and imperfect, that we are never able perfectly to fulfill the works of the law. Even after we are reborn, if we say that we have no sin, we deceive ourselves and the truth of God is not in us. It is therefore essential for us to lay hold on Christ Jesus, in his righteousness and his atonement, since he is the end and consummation of the Law and since it is by him that we are set at liberty so that the curse of God may not fall upon us, even though we do not fulfill the Law in all points. For as God the Father beholds us in the body of his Son Christ Jesus, he accepts our imperfect obedience as if it were perfect, and covers our works, which are defiled with many stains, with the righteousness of his Son. We do not mean that we are so set at liberty that we owe no obedience to the Law--for we have already acknowledged its place--but we affirm that no man on earth, with the sole exception of Christ Jesus, has given, gives, or shall give in action that obedience to the Law which the Law requires. When we have done all things we must fall down and unfeignedly confess that we are unprofitable servants. Therefore, whoever boasts of the merits of his own works or puts his trust in works of supererogation, boasts of what does not exist, and puts his trust in damnable idolatry.

Chapter 16 - The Kirk

As we believe in one God, Father, Son, and Holy Ghost, so we firmly believe that from the beginning there has been, now is, and to the end of the world shall be, one Kirk, that is to say, one company and multitude of men chosen by God, who rightly worship and embrace him by true faith in Jesus Christ, who is the only Head of the Kirk, even as it is the body and spouse of Christ Jesus. This Kirk is catholic, that is, universal, because it contains the chosen of all ages, of all realms, nations, and tongues, be they of the Jews or be they of the Gentiles, who have communion and society with God the Father, and with his Son, Christ Jesus, through the sanctification of his Holy Spirit. It is therefore called the communion, not of profane persons, but of saints, who, as citizens of the heavenly Jerusalem, have the fruit of inestimable benefits, one God, one Lord Jesus, one faith, and one baptism. Out of this Kirk there is neither life nor eternal felicity. Therefore we utterly abhor the blasphemy of those who hold that men who live according to equity and justice shall be saved, no matter what religion they profess. For since there is neither life nor salvation without Christ Jesus; so shall none have part therein but those whom the Father has given unto his Son Christ Jesus, and those who in time come to him, avow his doctrine, and believe in him. (We include the children with the believing parents.) This Kirk is invisible, known only to God, who alone knows whom he has chosen, and includes both the chosen who are departed, the Kirk triumphant, those who yet live and fight against sin and Satan, and those who shall live hereafter.

Chapter 17 - The Immortality of Souls

The chosen departed are in peace, and rest from their labors; not that they sleep and are lost in oblivion as some fanatics hold, for they are delivered from all fear and torment, and all the temptations to which we and all God's chosen are subject in this life, and because of which we are called the Kirk militant. On the other hand, the reprobate and unfaithful departed have anguish, torment, and pain which cannot be expressed. Neither the one nor the other is in such sleep that they feel no joy or torment, as is testified by Christ's parable in St. Luke XVI, his words to the thief, and the words of the souls crying under the altar, "O Lord, thou that art righteous and just, how long shalt thou not revenge our blood upon those that dwell in the earth?"

Chapter 18 - The Notes by Which the True Kirk Shall Be Determined From The False, and Who Shall Be Judge of Doctrine

Since Satan has labored from the beginning to adorn his pestilent synagogue with the title of the Kirk of God, and has incited cruel murderers to persecute, trouble, and molest the true Kirk and its members, as Cain did to Abel, Ishmael to Isaac, Esau to Jacob, and the whole priesthood of the Jews to Christ Jesus himself and his apostles after him. So it is essential that the true Kirk be distinguished from the filthy synagogues by clear and perfect notes lest we, being deceived, receive and embrace, to our own condemnation, the one for the other. The notes, signs, and assured tokens whereby the spotless bride of Christ is known from the horrible harlot, the false Kirk, we state, are neither antiquity, usurped title, lineal succession, appointed place, nor the numbers of men approving an error. For Cain was before Abel and Seth in age and title; Jerusalem had precedence above all other parts of the earth, for in it were priests lineally descended from Aaron, and greater numbers followed the scribes, Pharisees, and priests, than unfeignedly believed and followed Christ Jesus and his doctrine . . . and yet no man of judgment, we suppose, will hold that any of the forenamed were the Kirk of God. The notes of the true Kirk, therefore, we believe, confess, and avow to be: first, the true preaching of the Word of God, in which God has revealed himself to us, as the writings of the prophets and apostles declare; secondly, the right administration of the sacraments of Christ Jesus, with which must be associated the Word and promise of God to seal and confirm them in our hearts; and lastly, ecclesiastical discipline uprightly ministered, as God's Word prescribes, whereby vice is repressed and virtue nourished. Then wherever these notes are seen and continue for any time, be the number complete or not, there, beyond any doubt, is the true Kirk of Christ, who, according to his promise, is in its midst. This is not that universal Kirk of which we have spoken before, but particular Kirks, such as were in Corinth, Galatia, Ephesus, and other places where the ministry was planted by Paul and which he himself called Kirks of God. Such Kirks, we the inhabitants of the realm of Scotland confessing Christ Jesus, do claim to have in our cities, towns, and reformed districts because of the doctrine taught in our Kirks, contained in the written Word of God, that is, the Old and New Testaments, in those books which were originally reckoned as canonical. We affirm that in these all things necessary to be believed for the salvation of man are sufficiently expressed. The interpretation of Scripture, we confess, does not belong to any private or public person, nor yet to any Kirk for pre-eminence or precedence, personal or local, which it has above others, but pertains to the Spirit of God by whom the Scriptures were written. When controversy arises about the right understanding of any passage or sentence of Scripture, or for the reformation of any abuse within the Kirk of God, we ought not so much to ask what men have said or done before us, as what the Holy Ghost uniformly speaks within the body of the Scriptures and what Christ Jesus himself did and commanded. For it is agreed by all that the Spirit of God, who is the Spirit of unity, cannot contradict himself. So if the interpretation or opinion of any theologian, Kirk, or council, is contrary to the plain Word of God written in any other passage of the Scripture, it is most certain that this is not the true understanding and meaning of the Holy Ghost, although councils, realms, and nations have approved and received it. We dare not receive or admit any interpretation which is contrary to any principal point of our faith, or to any other plain text of Scripture, or to the rule of love.

Chapter 19 - The Authority of the Scriptures

As we believe and confess the Scriptures of God sufficient to instruct and make perfect the man of God, so do we affirm and avow their authority to be from God, and not to depend on men or angels. We affirm, therefore, that those who say the Scriptures have no other authority save that which they have received from the Kirk are blasphemous against God and injurious to the true Kirk, which always hears and obeys the voice of her own Spouse and Pastor, but takes not upon her to be mistress over the same.

Chapter 20 - General Councils, Their Power, Authority, and the Cause of Their Summoning

As we do not rashly condemn what good men, assembled together in general councils lawfully gathered, have set before us; so we do not receive uncritically whatever has been declared to men under the name of the general councils, for it is plain that, being human, some of them have manifestly erred, and that in matters of great weight and importance. So far then as the council confirms its decrees by the plain Word of God, so far do we reverence and embrace them. But if men, under the name of a council, pretend to forge for us new articles of faith, or to make decisions contrary to the Word of God, then we must utterly deny them as the doctrine of devils, drawing our souls from the voice of the one God to follow the doctrines and teachings of men. The reason why the general councils met was not to make any permanent law which God had not made before, nor yet to form new articles for our belief, nor to give the Word of God authority; much less to make that to be his Word, or even the true interpretation of it, which was not expressed previously by his holy will in his Word; but the reason for councils, at least of those that deserve that name, was partly to refute heresies, and to give public confession of their faith to the generations following, which they did by the authority of God's written Word, and not by any opinion or prerogative that they could not err by reason of their numbers. This, we judge, was the primary reason for general councils. The second was that good policy and order should be constitutes and observed in the Kirk where, as in the house of God, it becomes all things to be done decently and in order. Not that we think any policy of order of ceremonies can be appointed for all ages, times, and places; for as ceremonies which men have devised are but temporal, so they may, and ought to be, changed, when they foster superstition rather than edify the Kirk.

Chapter 21 - The Sacraments

As the fathers under the Law, besides the reality of the sacrifices, had two chief sacraments, that is, circumcision and the Passover, and those who rejected these were not reckoned among God's people; so do we acknowledge and confess that now in the time of the gospel we have two chief sacraments, which alone were instituted by the Lord Jesus and commanded to be used by all who will be counted members of his body, that is, Baptism and the Supper or Table of the Lord Jesus, also called the Communion of His Body and Blood. These sacraments, both of the Old Testament and of the New, were instituted by God not only to make a visible distinction between his people and those who were without the Covenant, but also to exercise the faith of his children and, by participation of these sacraments, to seal in their hearts the assurance of his promise, and of that most blessed conjunction, union, and society, which the chosen have with their Head, Christ Jesus. And so we utterly condemn the vanity of those who affirm the sacraments to be nothing else than naked and bare signs. No, we assuredly believe that by Baptism we are engrafted into Christ Jesus, to be made partakers of his righteousness, by which our sins are covered and remitted, and also that in the Supper rightly used, Christ Jesus is so joined with us that he becomes the very nourishment and food for our souls. Not that we imagine any transubstantiation of bread into Christ's body, and of wine into his natural blood, as the Romanists have perniciously taught and wrongly believed; but this union and conjunction which we have with the body and blood of Christ Jesus in the right use of the sacraments is wrought by means of the Holy Ghost, who by true faith carries us above all things that are visible, carnal, and earthly, and makes us feed upon the body and blood of Christ Jesus, once broken and shed for us but now in heaven, and appearing for us in the presence of his Father. Notwithstanding the distance between his glorified body in heaven and mortal men on earth, yet we must assuredly believe that the bread which we break is the communion of Christ's body and the cup which we bless the communion of his blood. Thus we confess and believe without doubt that the faithful, in the right use of the Lord's Table, do so eat the body and drink the blood of the Lord Jesus that he remains in them and they in him; they are so made flesh of his flesh and bone of his bone that as the eternal Godhood has given to the flesh of Christ Jesus, which by nature was corruptible and mortal, life and immortality, so the eating and drinking of the flesh and blood of Christ Jesus does the like for us. We grant that this is neither given to us merely at the time nor by the power and virtue of the sacrament alone, but we affirm that the faithful, in the right use of the Lord's Table, have such union with Christ Jesus as the natural man cannot apprehend. Further we affirm that although the faithful, hindered by negligence and human weakness, do not profit as much as they ought in the actual moment of the Supper, yet afterwards it shall bring forth fruit, being living seed sown in good ground; for the Holy Spirit, who can never be separated from the right institution of the Lord Jesus, will not deprive the faithful of the fruit of that mystical action. Yet all this, we say again, comes of that true faith which apprehends Christ Jesus, who alone makes the sacrament effective in us. Therefore, if anyone slanders us by saying that we affirm or believe the sacraments to be symbols and nothing more, they are libelous and speak against the plain facts. On the other hand we readily admit that we make a distinction between Christ Jesus in his eternal substance and the elements of the sacramental signs. So we neither worship the elements, in place of that which they signify, nor yet do we despise them or undervalue them, but we use them with great reverence, examining ourselves diligently before we participate, since we are assured by the mouth of the apostle that "whoever shall eat this bread, and drink this cup of the Lord, unworthily, shall be guilty of the body and blood of the Lord."

Chapter 22 - The Right Administration of the Sacraments

Two things are necessary for the right administration of the sacraments. The first is that they should be ministered by lawful ministers, and we declare that these are men appointed to preach the Word, unto whom God has given the power to preach the gospel, and who are lawfully called by some Kirk. The second is that they should be ministered in the elements and manner which God has appointed. Otherwise they cease to be the sacraments of Christ Jesus. This is why we abandon the teaching of the Roman Church and withdraw from its sacraments; firstly, because their ministers are not true ministers of Christ Jesus (indeed they even allow women, whom the Holy Ghost will not permit to preach in the congregation to baptize) and, secondly, because they have so adulterated both the sacraments with their own additions that no part of Christ's original act remains in its original simplicity. The addition of oil, salt, spittle, and such like in baptism, are merely human additions. To adore or venerate the sacrament, to carry it through streets and towns in procession, or to reserve it in a special case, is not the proper use of Christ's sacrament but an abuse of it. Christ Jesus said, "Take ye, eat ye," and "Do this in remembrance of Me." By these words and commands he sanctified bread and wine to be the sacrament of his holy body and blood, so that the one should be eaten and that all should drink of the other, and not that they should be reserved for worship or honored as God, as the Romanists do. Further, in withdrawing one part of the sacrament--the blessed cup--from the people, they have committed sacrilege. Moreover, if the sacraments are to be rightly used it is essential that the end and purpose of their institution should be understood, not only by the minister but also by the recipients. For if the recipient does not understand what is being done, the sacrament is not being rightly used, as is seen in the case of the Old Testament sacrifices. Similarly, if the teacher teaches false doctrine which is hateful to God, even though the sacraments are his own ordinance, they are not rightly used, since wicked men have used them for another end than what God had commanded. We affirm that this has been done to the sacraments in the Roman Church, for there the whole action of the Lord Jesus is adulterated in form, purpose, and meaning. What Christ Jesus did, and commanded to be done, is evident from the Gospels and from St. Paul; what the priest does at the altar we do not need to tell. The end and purpose of Christ's institution, for which it should be used, is set forth in the words, "Do this in remembrance of Me," and "For as often as ye eat this bread and drink this cup ye do show"--that is, extol, preach, magnify, and praise--"the Lord's death, till He come." But let the words of the mass, and their own doctors and teachings witness, what is the purpose and meaning of the mass; it is that, as mediators between Christ and his Kirk, they should offer to God the Father, a sacrifice in propitiation for the sins of the living and of the dead. This doctrine is blasphemous to Christ Jesus and would deprive his unique sacrifice, once offered on the cross for the cleansing of all who are to be sanctified, of its sufficiency; so we detest and renounce it.

Chapter 23 - To Whom Sacraments Appertain

We hold that baptism applies as much to the children of the faithful as to those who are of age and discretion, and so we condemn the error of the Anabaptists, who deny that children should be baptized before they have faith and understanding. But we hold that the Supper of the Lord is only for those who are of the household of faith and can try and examine themselves both in their faith and their duty to their neighbors. Those who eat and drink at that holy table without faith, or without peace and goodwill to their brethren, eat unworthily. This is the reason why ministers in our Kirk make public and individual examination of those who are to be admitted to the table of the Lord Jesus.

Chapter 24 - The Civil Magistrate

We confess and acknowledge that empires, kingdoms, dominions, and cities are appointed and ordained by God; the powers and authorities in them, emperors in empires, kings in their realms, dukes and princes in their dominions, and magistrates in cities, are ordained by God's holy ordinance for the manifestation of his own glory and for the good and well being of all men. We hold that any men who conspire to rebel or to overturn the civil powers, as duly established, are not merely enemies to humanity but rebels against God's will. Further, we confess and acknowledge that such persons as are set in authority are to be loved, honored, feared, and held in the highest respect, because they are the lieutenants of God, and in their councils God himself doth sit and judge. They are the judges and princes to whom God has given the sword for the praise and defense of good men and the punishment of all open evil doers. Moreover, we state the preservation and purification of religion is particularly the duty of kings, princes, rulers, and magistrates. They are not only appointed for civil government but also to maintain true religion and to suppress all idolatry and superstition. This may be seen in David, Jehosaphat, Hezekiah, Josiah, and others highly commended for their zeal in that cause.

Therefore we confess and avow that those who resist the supreme powers, so long as they are acting in their own spheres, are resisting God's ordinance and cannot be held guiltless. We further state that so long as princes and rulers vigilantly fulfill their office, anyone who denies them aid, counsel, or service, denies it to God, who by his lieutenant craves it of them.

Chapter 25 - The Gifts Freely Given to the Kirk

Although the Word of God truly preached, the sacraments rightly ministered, and discipline executed according to the Word of God, are certain and infallible signs of the true Kirk, we do not mean that every individual person in that company is a chosen member of Christ Jesus. We acknowledge and confess that many weeds and tares are sown among the corn and grow in great abundance in its midst, and that the reprobate may be found in the fellowship of the chosen and may take an outward part with them in the benefits of the Word and sacraments. But since they only confess God for a time with their mouths but not with their hearts, they lapse, and do not continue to the end. Therefore they do not share the fruits of Christ's death, resurrection, and ascension. But such as unfeignedly believe with the heart and boldly confess the Lord Jesus with their mouths shall certainly receive his gifts. Firstly, in this life, they shall receive remission of sins and that be faith in Christ's blood alone; for though sin shall remain and continually abide in our mortal bodies, yet it shall not be counted against us, but be pardoned, and covered with Christ's righteousness. Secondly, in the general judgment, there shall be given to every man and woman resurrection of the flesh. The seas shall give up her dead, and the earth those who are buried within her. Yea, the Eternal, our God, shall stretch out his hand on the dust, and the dead shall arise incorruptible, and in the very substance of the selfsame flesh which every man now bears, to receive according to their works, glory or punishment. Such as now delight in vanity, cruelty, filthiness, superstition, or idolatry, shall be condemned to the fire unquenchable, in which those who now serve the devil in all abominations shall be tormented forever, both in body and in spirit. But such as continue in well doing to the end, boldly confessing the Lord Jesus, shall receive glory, honor, and immortality, we constantly believe, to reign forever in life everlasting with Christ Jesus, to whose glorified body all his chosen shall be made like, when he shall appear again in judgment and shall render up the Kingdom to God his Father, who then shall be and ever shall remain, all in all things, God blessed forever. To whom, with the Son and the Holy Ghost, be all honor and glory, now and ever. Amen.

Arise, O Lord, and let thine enemies be confounded; let them flee from thy presence that hate thy godly Name. Give thy servants strength to speak thy Word with boldness, and let all nations cleave to the true knowledge of thee. Amen.

Made in the USA
Lexington, KY
04 April 2018